MW01140070

Let's Celebrate

WOMEN'S EQUALITY DAY

BY Barbara deRubertis

Kane Press
New York

> # For activities and resources for this book and others in the HOLIDAYS & HEROES series, visit:
> ## www.kanepress.com/holidays-and-heroes

Text copyright © 2018 by Barbara deRubertis
Photographs/images copyrights: Cover: © Everett Historical/Shutterstock; page 1: © Gelpi/Shutterstock; page 3: © Ron Nickel/Design Pics/Newscom; page 4: © Howard Chandler Christy/Architect of the Capitol; page 5: © Harper's weekly. v.24 1880/HathiTrust Digital Library; page 6: © Library of Congress, Prints and Photographs Division, LC-USZ62-48965; page 7 top: © Library of Congress, Prints and Photographs Division, LC-USZ62-133477; page 7 inset: © National Portrait Gallery, Smithsonian Institution; page 8: © Granger Historical Archive; page 9: © National Portrait Gallery, Smithsonian Institution; page 10: © Library of Congress, Prints and Photographs Division, LC-USZ62-135681; page 11: © Glasshouse Images/Alamy Stock Photo; page 12: © Ilene MacDonald/Alamy Stock Photo; page 12 inset: © Ivy Close Images/Alamy Stock Photo; page 14 left: © Library of Congress, Prints and Photographs Division, LC-USZ62-93552; page 14 right: © Library of Congress, Prints and Photographs Division, mnwp000378; page 15: © Library of Congress, Prints and Photographs Division, LC-DIG-pga-02587; page 16 left: © Library of Congress, Prints and Photographs Division, LC-B2- 2667-6; page 16 right: © National Archives/NARA; page 17: © Library of Congress, Prints and Photographs Division, LC-USZ61-791; page 18: © Schomburg Center for Research in Black Culture/Jean Blackwell Hutson Research and Reference Division/The New York Public Library; page 18 inset: © Library of Congress, Prints and Photographs Division, LC-USZ62-54722; page 19: © National Portrait Gallery, Smithsonian Institution; page 20: © Library of Congress, Prints and Photographs Division, LC-H27- A-1112; page 21: © Library of Congress, Prints and Photographs Division, LC-H261- 6303; page 22: ©Jejim/Shutterstock; page 23 top: © Courtesy of Tennessee State Library and Archives; page 23 bottom: © Chronicling America: Historic American Newspapers, Library of Congress; page 24 top: ©Everett Historical/Shutterstock; page 24 bottom: © Chronicling America: Historic American Newspapers, Library of Congress; page 25: ©Everett Historical/Shutterstock; page 26: © Giraphics/Shutterstock; page 27: © Joesph C. Garza/The Tribune-Star/Associated Press; page 28: © Joyce Boghosian/Zuma Press/Newscom; page 29: © Fizkes/Shutterstock; page 30: ©Vector Brothers/Shutterstock; page 31: © Adam Fenster/Reuters/Newscom; page 32 top: © Library of Congress, Prints and Photographs Division, LC-USZ62-135533; page 32 middle: © Tetra Images/Alamy Stock Photo; page 32 bottom: ©Holly Vegter/Shutterstock, back cover: © Gelpi/Shutterstock
All due diligence has been conducted in identifying copyright holders and obtaining permissions.

All rights reserved. No part of this book may be reproduced or transmitted in any form or by any means, electronic or mechanical, including photocopying, recording, or by any information storage and retrieval system, without permission in writing from the publisher. For information regarding permission, contact the publisher through its website: www.kanepress.com.

Library of Congress Cataloging-in-Publication Data

Names: deRubertis, Barbara, author.
Title: Let's celebrate Women's equality day / by Barbara deRubertis.
Description: New York : Kane Press, [2018] | Series: Holidays & heroes |
  Audience: Age: 6-10.
Identifiers: LCCN 2017051920 (print) | LCCN 2017053213 (ebook) | ISBN
  9781635920659 (ebook) | ISBN 9781635920635 (reinforced library binding : alk.
  paper) | ISBN 9781635920642 (pbk. : alk. paper)
Subjects: LCSH: Women's rights--United States--Juvenile literature. |
  Women--Legal status, laws, etc.--United States--Juvenile literature. |
  Women--United States--History--Juvenile literature.
Classification: LCC HQ1236.5.U6 (ebook) | LCC HQ1236.5.U6 D47 2018 (print) |
  DDC 323.3/40973--dc23
LC record available at https://lccn.loc.gov/2017051920

10 9 8 7 6 5 4 3 2 1

First published in the United States of America in 2018 by Kane Press, Inc.
Printed in China

Book Design and Photograph/Image Research: Maura Taboubi

Visit us online at **www.kanepress.com**.

Like us on Facebook
facebook.com/kanepress

Follow us on Twitter
@KanePress

For over a hundred years, women in the United States fought for the right to vote. Without it, they had no voice in their own government. They had no say in how the country was run!

Many American women devoted their entire lives to working for women's "suffrage," or the right to vote. They wanted voting rights that were equal to men's! Women finally won this right in 1920. But their struggle began long before.

In 1787, the new U.S. Constitution let the states decide who would be allowed to vote. Most states decided that the only people who could vote had to be:

- white
- male
- Protestant
- property owners
- tax payers
- over the age of 21

The Constitutional Convention, 1787

From 1787–1807, women were allowed to vote in New Jersey.

In four states, freed male slaves could vote.

In New Jersey, the law did not say that only men could vote. So some women did . . . for a few years. Then the state took that right away.

When George Washington was elected president in 1789, only about 1% of the population cast votes.

An Event of Great Importance: The Seneca Falls Women's Rights Convention

Elizabeth Cady Stanton was called a "suffragist" because she fought for women's suffrage. She argued strongly that women should have the right to:

- own property
- keep the money they earn
- receive a college education
- obtain a divorce
- vote
- hold public office

Elizabeth Cady Stanton and her daughter Harriot

The 1840 World Anti-Slavery Convention where
Stanton met Lucretia Mott

Lucretia Mott

Stanton was also an
"abolitionist." She supported the abolition—
or end—of slavery. Years earlier, she had met
another abolitionist, Lucretia Mott, at an anti-
slavery convention. Together they organized the
first women's rights convention. It was held in
Seneca Falls, New York, in 1848.

Elizabeth Cady Stanton presented a "Declaration" at this convention. She listed many ways in which women were treated unfairly. She asked for more rights and better treatment. Then she boldly demanded women's right to vote.

Lucretia Mott wanted this demand removed. She thought it went too far.

Elizabeth Cady Stanton speaks at the Seneca Falls convention in 1848.

Frederick Douglass

But a former slave named Frederick Douglass supported the idea. He had become a famous speaker, writer, and thinker. And his powerful speech in support of women's suffrage helped win people over! So Stanton's declaration was accepted.

Men shout at a women's rights convention.

The first *national* women's rights convention was held in 1850. Another was held in 1851. But some men came to cause trouble. They said women were weaker than men in body, mind, and spirit—so women shouldn't have the right to vote.

That didn't sit well with former slave and abolitionist Sojourner Truth! Six feet tall, with strong muscles and a powerful voice, she rose from her seat. She gave a short, passionate speech that won over the crowd to the idea of women's suffrage. It was a speech that people remembered for years to come.

She said, "I am as strong as any man." Everyone could see that Sojourner spoke the *truth*!

Sojourner Truth

A statue in Seneca Falls shows Amelia Bloomer introducing Elizabeth Cady Stanton and Susan B. Anthony.

Susan B. Anthony

Also in 1851, Elizabeth Cady Stanton met Susan B. Anthony. Anthony had read a speech by Stanton and was inspired to become a suffragist. These two women worked together for the next 50 years.

In 1865, the Civil War ended and slaves became free. Anthony, Stanton, and Truth took a stand that shocked many people. They opposed the 15th Amendment to the Constitution, which would grant African American men the right to vote!

What? WHY?

They believed African American *men* should not be given the right to vote ahead of white and black *women*.

Like many women then, they believed in "universal suffrage." They thought the right to vote should be granted to men *and* women, white *and* black, at the same time. They worked for this kind of amendment to the Constitution.

The American Woman Suffrage Association (AWSA) published its own magazine, the *Woman's Journal,* edited by Lucy Stone.

The National Woman Suffrage Association (NWSA) was founded by Stanton and Anthony.

So, in 1869, the women's suffrage movement split. Stanton and Anthony's group supported universal suffrage. The other group supported first passing the 15th Amendment and giving men the right to vote regardless of race or color. This group planned to get voting rights for women later—one state at a time.

The 15th Amendment passed in 1870. In the years following, enormous struggles over women's suffrage took place.

African American men in Baltimore celebrate the passing of the 15th Amendment, 1870.

A PETITION FOR UNIVERSAL SUFFRAGE.

To the Senate and House of Representatives:

The undersigned, Women of the United States, respectfully ask an amendment of the Constitution that shall prohibit the several States from disfranchising any of their citizens on the ground of sex.

In making our demand for Suffrage, we would call your attention to the fact that we represent fifteen million people—one half the entire population of the country—intelligent, virtuous, native-born American citizens; and yet stand outside the pale of political recognition.

The Constitution classes us as "free people," and counts us *whole* persons in the basis of representation; and yet are we governed without our consent, compelled to pay taxes without appeal, and punished for violations of law without choice of judge or juror.

The experience of all ages, the Declarations of the Fathers, the Statute Laws of our own day, and the fearful revolution through which we have just passed, all prove the uncertain tenure of life, liberty and property so long as the ballot—the only weapon of self-protection—is not in the hand of every citizen.

Therefore, as you are now amending the Constitution, and, in harmony with advancing civilization, placing new safeguards round the individual rights of four millions of emancipated slaves, we ask that you extend the right of Suffrage to Woman—the only remaining class of disfranchised citizens—and thus fulfil your Constitutional obligation "to Guarantee to every State in the Union a Republican form of Government."

As all partial application of Republican principles must ever breed a complicated legislation as well as a discontented people, we would pray your Honorable Body, in order to simplify the machinery of government and ensure domestic tranquillity, that you legislate hereafter for persons, citizens, tax-payers, and not for class or caste.

For justice and equality your petitioners will ever pray.

NAMES.	RESIDENCE.
Elizabeth Stanton,	New York
Susan B. Anthony	Rochester—N.Y.

Stanton and Anthony were the first to sign this petition for universal suffrage.

A woman holds a banner with a Susan B. Anthony quote: "Failure is impossible."

Susan B. Anthony became more and more *determined* and *bold*. For example:

She was arrested for illegally voting in 1872.

She also refused to pay the judge's fine. (Her lawyer paid it.)

She filed petitions with 10,000 signatures.

She asked every Congress from 1869 to 1906 to pass a women's suffrage amendment.

Finally, after 18 years, the two women's rights groups that had split apart joined together again in 1887. They decided they were stronger when they worked as one.

Elizabeth Cady Stanton was elected president. Susan B. Anthony was vice president.

These two women never, ever gave up. Sadly, neither of them lived to see women win the right to vote.

Stanton died in 1902, Anthony in 1906.

When the NWSA and AWSA joined together again, they became the National American Woman Suffrage Association (NAWSA). Stanton and Anthony were president and vice president.

Around this time, prominent African American women became important leaders in the suffrage movement. They saw that they faced even greater difficulties than white women. And they didn't always have the support they needed from the larger women's groups. So they organized new clubs.

The National Association of Colored Women (NACW) was founded in 1896 by Harriet Tubman, Frances E.W. Harper, Ida B. Wells, and Mary Church Terrell (right). Terrell became the NACW's first president.

Ida B. Wells

Ida B. Wells founded the first of these clubs, the Alpha Suffrage Club, in Chicago in 1913. Wells had become famous for writing about the unfair and inhumane treatment of African Americans.

Because of her race, she was once told to march in the back of a suffrage parade. She refused! She marched right alongside the white women. She wanted to show that black women were just as important as white women in the fight for voting rights.

Alice Paul flies the victory banner from suffrage headquarters, 1920.

Finally, in 1920, women achieved a huge
victory. Congress passed the 19th Amendment
to the U.S. Constitution. If approved, this
amendment would at last give women the right
to vote.

Why Did Congress Finally Support Women's Right to Vote?

Alice Paul

• By 1910, most western states had begun to give full or limited voting rights to women.

• In 1916, the U.S. entered the First World War. Women worked hard to support the war effort. People realized how valuable their help was!

• A young woman named Alice Paul became a courageous leader of the fight for a constitutional amendment. She and other suffragists were arrested and thrown in jail. They protested by refusing to eat. So they were force fed by their jailers. These events stirred up a lot of sympathy.

• The 19th Amendment was introduced in Congress in 1918. This time the President—Woodrow Wilson—openly supported it.

But the fight wasn't over. The 19th Amendment now had to be "ratified," or approved, by three-fourths of the states. Tennessee was in line to become the necessary 36th of the 48 states. Everyone knew that State Senator Harry T. Burn planned to vote "no." He was against the amendment.

Then Burn received a letter from his mother. She told him to "vote for suffrage." She wrote, "Don't forget to be a good boy. . . . With lots of love, Mama."

Top right: Harry T. Burn
Lower right: A newspaper headline from 1920
Left: A monument to women's suffrage in Tennessee

An American woman casts her vote, 1920.

On August 18, 1920, the vote was held. When Burn's turn came up, the count was tied, 48 to 48. Burn's vote would break the tie. But Burn had changed his mind. Holding his mother's letter, he voted "yes"!

This meant that the 19th Amendment was now approved by 36 states. So ALL women in ALL states would have the right to vote!

One week later, the 19th Amendment was adopted—on **August 26, 1920**. Fifty years later, this important date would be chosen for Women's Equality Day.

But Alice Paul knew that the right to vote wasn't enough. Women needed full equal rights. Paul announced that she would now work for an Equal Rights Amendment. And she did so for the rest of her life.

Members of the National League of Women Voters, 1924

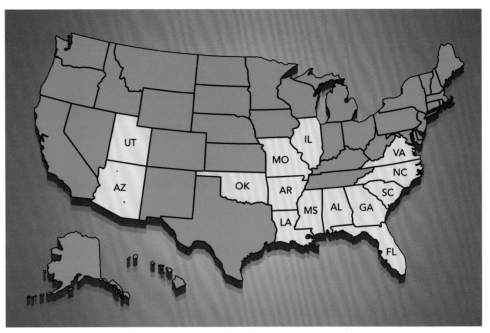

As of 2017, the states in yellow had not yet ratified the ERA.

The Equal Rights Amendment

In 1923, the Equal Rights Amendment (ERA) was introduced in Congress. This amendment would not allow people's rights to be limited or denied because of their gender.

It took until 1972 for Congress to pass the ERA. But 38 of the 50 states were required to ratify it.

As of 2017, 36 states had ratified the amendment. Two more are needed . . . just two more. Has your state ratified the ERA?

Women's Equality Day in the U.S. and International Women's Day

In 1971, Congress named **August 26** Women's Equality Day. Every president since then has issued a proclamation on this day honoring women and their struggles for equality.

Also, in 1975, the United Nations recognized worldwide concerns about women's rights. So it named **March 8** International Women's Day. Every year the celebrations of women's achievements grow larger. And calls for more gender equality grow louder!

A young girl marches for women's equality.

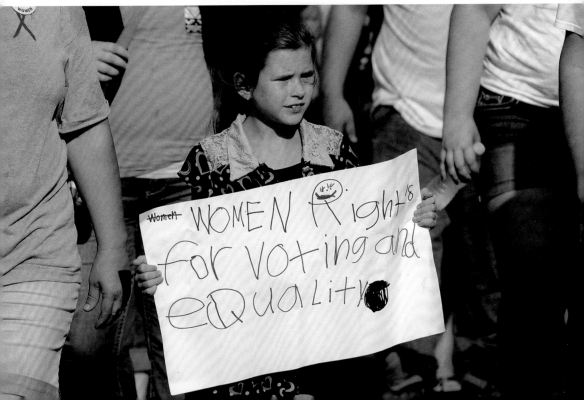

The Gender Gap in Political Offices

Over the last 100 years, more and more women have been elected to political offices. But, as of 2017, there were still far fewer women than men in Congress. Only 104 of the 435 members were women.

And, as of 2017, a woman had not yet been elected President or Vice President of the United States.

A photo of Congress, 2018

The Gender Gap in Business

A study in 2014 found that women, on average, earn less money than men—even when they do the same job.

In the 500 largest businesses in the U.S., there are 2,500 people holding the top five jobs. At this time, only 350 of them are women.

Men still hold more of the top jobs than women.

How Can We Celebrate Women's Equality Day in the U.S. and International Women's Day?

Read and learn more about the women's suffrage movement. Read about women's ongoing struggle for equal rights, equal pay, and equal opportunities.

Ask people you know—men as well as women—to sign a petition to make Women's Equality Day a federal holiday in the U.S.

Make a poster for Women's Equality Day on August 26 and for International Women's Day on March 8. Post them on your front door!

Remind the women you know to VOTE!

March 8 • August 26

The grave of Susan B. Anthony on Election Day, 2016

On Election Day in 2016, hundreds of women came to the cemetery where Susan B. Anthony is buried. Some visited cemeteries where other suffragists are buried. The visitors left flowers and "I voted" stickers at the suffragists' graves.

The women who visited these graves knew they owed all the suffragists a huge debt of gratitude. This was their way of saying "thank you."

There have been a great many women who have done a great deal of work to give women rights that are equal to men's rights in America.

Some of these women are still famous. There are many more whose names are no longer remembered. When we celebrate Women's Equality Day, we celebrate ALL of these women and ALL of their contributions.

But the work is not done. It continues today. And we can help!